Van Johnson's
HOLLYWOOD
A Family Album

SHANNONGROVE
PRESS

Van Johnson's
HOLLYWOOD
A Family Album

Memories by **SCHUYLER JOHNSON**

Photographs & Stories by **EVIE WYNN JOHNSON**

Introduction by **CARLETON VARNEY**

CONTENTS

My sister Vivian and I spent many a Saturday at the Paramount Theater in Lynn, Massachusetts, watching double features.

Introduction

A Family Album from Hollywood's Golden Years

by CARLETON VARNEY

The "Golden Age" of Hollywood. When MGM, Paramount, Warner Brothers and 20th Century Fox ran everything, from their own theaters across America to the lives of their movie stars. The glamour of the 1930s, '40s and '50s was available to anyone for the price of a ticket to their city or town's cinema.

An afternoon double feature was certainly an event in the Boston suburb of Lynn, Massachusetts, where I grew up. We had five movie theaters, including the Paramount, the Warner and the Capital. News of the world opened each show, and the seats were always filled. I was a Betty Grable junkie, so whenever a film featuring the lady with the million dollar legs was playing at the movie house (*The Dolly Sisters, Springtime in the Rockies*), I was there to watch. As the 1950s melted into the '60s and '70s, the Golden Age of television was upon us, and it began to take over family entertainment—one didn't even have to leave the house now. Also over were my radio days spent listening to *Lux Presents Hollywood* and my favorite shows, *The Phantom* and *Nick Carter, Master Detective*.

Van Johnson was a top box office success for MGM in 1947 and 1948, but he and I would meet later. Destiny introduced me to Hollywood, Broadway and television people, including a pillar of interior design, the great Dorothy Draper. When the decorating house Dorothy Draper & Company, Inc. became my very permanent home—which it still is—I began my *own* on-camera life, first on ABC's *Midday Live* in New York City; then at CBN with my show *Inside Design;* and most recently during my five-year run at HSN's *Live Vividly*.

Luckily, I had coaching from the best of the Golden Age of Hollywood stars. Joan Crawford, my client and friend for almost 20 years, advised me on how to dress for a decorating show pilot. It was Joan who introduced me to Van Johnson. On screen, Van was the Pied Piper; he was Judy Garland's love in *The Good Old Summertime*; he was a war pilot with Spencer Tracy in *A Guy Named Joe*; he romanced Elizabeth Taylor in *The Last Time I Saw Paris*; and he wooed bathing beauty Esther Williams in half a dozen pictures. He was America's boy next door, but he became my friend and client for many years.

We had long talks and frequently saw each other for dinner (or to look at a cranberry English toile fabric I was suggesting), a trip to a museum, or a gallery opening. He even wanted to turn my son Nicholas into a movie star! After Van passed away, I took on a bit of his style. I only wear red socks, morning, noon and night, in his memory.

Here is a photograph I keep on a wall in the living room of my home in Ireland. Van signed it with the inscription: "For Carleton. We've come a long way together. Peace, Van." And indeed we have—right to the pages of this book—one that honors his loving character.

I did not see Van after he moved from his penthouse apartment on East 54th Street in New York City to the Tappan Zee Manor assisted-living facility on the Hudson River in New York toward the end of his life. He had difficulty hearing and just wanted—like Greta Garbo—to be alone with his books, needlepoint and memories. Van was always creative—not only an actor, singer and dancer, but a painter, decorator, and lover of beautiful things and kind people. He had grown up in Newport, Rhode Island, with his father, who was a plumber and later a real-estate salesman, so Van had visited the many mansions of that illustrious seacoast town.

I read about Van's death on December 12, 2008, on *The New York Times* obituary page. I attempted to contact his daughter, Schuyler, but wasn't able to find her. I did track her down eventually, and visited her in Florida, hoping to locate some of Van's many artistic endeavors, especially a painting he had done of Diana Vreeland's red-on-red New York apartment. Schuyler Johnson was not living as she once had—in a Hollywood mansion with a swimming pool and celebrated neighbors. Nor is she related to Don Johnson or his movie-star daughter, Dakota. She is the 67-year-old daughter of an actor loved

by a generation addicted to Turner Classic Movies. Schuyler is a woman of strength looking to reestablish the connection with her father that was lost in an acrimonious divorce. Her mother, Evie Wynn Johnson, did not want Schuyler to have contact with her father after the separation. From age 14 to 48, she saw him in person only twice. The final time was at his hotel suite in Florida, where he was appearing on stage in a revue. While she was not able to spend much time with her father that night, she did receive a final embrace.

Van Johnson was a sensitive actor—a man who couldn't abide confrontation of any sorts. I knew and understood his feelings well. Van loved his daughter. He spoke of her fondly over the years, but he never contacted her, I believe out of the desire to avoid confronting his ex-wife.

Schuyler showed me this scrapbook album during our very first meeting. As we sat on a bench in front of her modest home in Lake Worth, Florida, I marveled at the candid pictures, many taken by Evie and accompanied by her notations. Schuyler's family's story is simply amazing. With this book, she passes along an intimate view of her father's life and legacy—as well as her mother's—to fans of Hollywood's Golden Age.

Van and I together opening night of *Stairway to the Stars* at the London Palladium. I had designed the stage set for the production, which Van starred in.

Van and daughter Schuyler together in happy days,
when they would take long walks together.

Memories

by SCHUYLER JOHNSON

MY PARENTS

Van Johnson was a big man for his era—6 foot 3 inches—but he never gave the impression of being too tall. He was just right. He had an incredible grace about him; he moved like a dancer. He loved cologne and had huge bottles in every bathroom. I can still remember the bottle in the downstairs powder room, which had a beautiful hunting scene painted on it, and a wooden stopper. He had hangers specially made that looked like gigantic shoulders, and kept them neatly lined up in his closet, a room that was as large as a small bedroom.

He used a pine-scented bubble bath, and wore red socks, which he washed out each night, turning the water pink. He favored Kent hairbrushes. The largest brush had whalebone bristles—very long and very strong; he would sometimes brush my hair with it, leaving furrows in my scalp.

Every Sunday Van and I would ride to church in his black Cadillac Fleetwood, me wearing white gloves, my hair pulled back so tightly that my face felt stretched. Afterwards we would go to the Beverly Hills Hotel coffee shop and indulge in freshly squeezed orange juice and buttermilk pancakes, and then to the hotel magazine shop where he would buy me any book I wanted. Toys were for Christmas and birthdays, but I could have books by the truckload. Even after he left, he always sent me books, along with a letter signed with his happy-face signature.

At Christmastime, before my parents' marriage ended, he and I would walk through Beverly Hills looking at the shop windows. We came to a furniture store once where a mannequin children's choir was on display; for some reason, it scared me to death—I thought they looked like dead children—but I did not voice this to my father, who loved it.

Walks were mandatory. After dinner, no matter where we were, we would walk for hours; I skipped to keep up. In Switzerland (more on that later) we would take rolls from our dinner and go down to the lake to feed the swans. One of them became so enamored of us (or the rolls) that he followed us all the way back to the hotel.

◆ ◆ ◆

In the 1940s and 1950s, homosexuality and bisexuality were strictly verboten. Like the Salem Witch Trials or the McCarthy hearings, even a whiff of gossip could permanently derail careers in Hollywood. When rumors started about Rock Hudson, the studio decided that his friend, actor George Nader, would be "thrown to the wolves" in order to save Hudson's career, a favor that Hudson repaid by leaving Nader the income from his estate when he died.

Before my parents were married, there were starting to be whispers about Van. He was summoned, along with Evie Wynn, into Louis B. Mayer's office, where Mayer offered a "suggestion" that Evie divorce her husband, Keenan Wynn (whom she had met while they were both doing summer stock in Maine), and marry Van. Van was close friends with the two of them, and although Evie felt a huge attraction to Van, it

Evie Wynn Johnson in Switzerland, circa 1954. An actress herself, she divorced her first husband, Keenan Wynn, to marry Van Johnson.

was hard to hurt Keenan. She and Keenan had been married for nine years and had two sons, Tracy and Ned; but they got a quickie divorce in Mexico, and Van and Evie were married that same year, 1947. Keenan and Van maintained their friendship even though I think Van was twisted with guilt over having hurt his old friend.

Given the circumstances that forced them into marriage, Evie and Van had a lot of fun, a lot of love, and a lot in common for a long time. Both had a fantastic sense of humor and a love for animals, as well as a passion for travel and painting.

✦ ✦ ✦

While Van was my sun, my excitement, Evie was my rock, my security, my dependable guardian. After Van left, she was there for us. Evie was tall—about 5 foot 8 inches—a brunette and very beautiful. She took great care in her appearance, and her clothes were always impeccable, even if she was only going to the mailbox. She had grown up in a large family, one of nine, with loving parents. Van had grown up with a detached father; his mother left when he was just two. There was virtually no love at all. Although I always felt my grandfather did love Van, he had no idea how to show it.

Van Johnson grew up in Newport, Rhode Island.

Van blossomed once he got away from his father's cold, loveless house and went to New York and Broadway. Admiration and love from live theater audiences compensated somewhat for those lost years.

When Van hit it big in the movies, Grandfather Johnson came out to California. Van and Evie took him to expensive restaurants where he ordered only tuna fish sandwiches. It drove Van crazy. He wanted to show his father he was a success, but his father resented it, supposedly because Van had not done what he wanted him to do—become a concert violinist—and this was his retribution.

Evie, however, settled happily into her new role as Mrs. Van Johnson, a title she maintained for the rest of her life, even after the divorce. She and Van got on very well for many years; he was the star, the breadwinner, and she was the manager, the hostess, the wife.

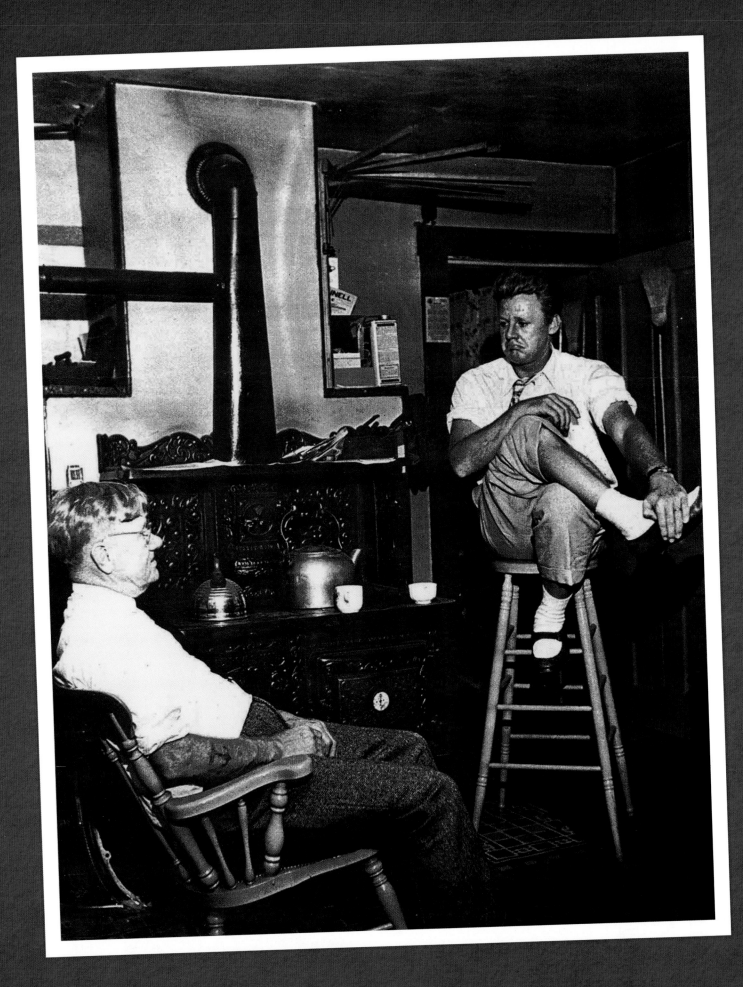

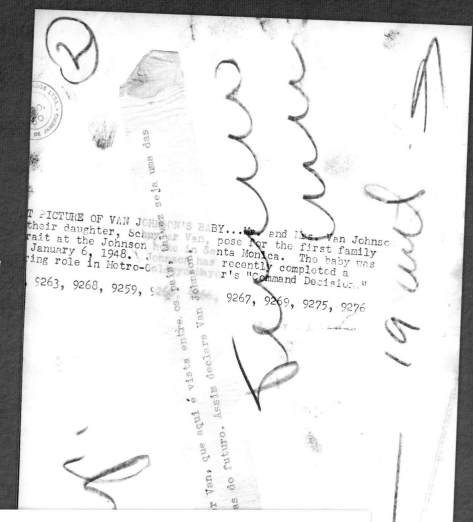

T PICTURE OF VAN JOHNSON'S BABY...Mr. and Mrs. Van Johnson
their daughter, Schuyler Van, pose for the first family
rait at the Johnson home in Santa Monica. The baby was
January 6, 1948. Johnson has recently completed a
ring role in Metro-Goldwyn-Mayer's "Command Decision."

9263, 9268, 9259, 9267, 9269, 9275, 9276

OPPOSITE

Van Johnson and his father at home in Newport, Rhode Island, in a photograph from *Look* magazine. Van never lost his New England style and way of life. Ship wheels, pine, and cranberry-colored toile fabric would be around his home for a lifetime.

RIGHT AND BELOW

Van, Schuyler and Evie Johnson shown in an MGM publicity photograph at the first Johnson home in Santa Monica.

AT HOME IN HOLLYWOOD

801 North Foothill Road, our home in Beverly Hills, was an enchanted place—
a child's dream with a huge backyard, pool, rose gardens and an apartment over the
garage. There was a lot to explore. There were two stained glass windows, one on
the landing of the front staircase, comprised of circles in all different colors—which
I would often look through and envision as purple, blue, green and yellow worlds—
and one in the library depicting St. George slaying the dragon. We all did some form
of art: Van and Tracy painted; Evie, Ned and I drew. We did most of our activities on
the patio (or the lanai, as Evie called it) by the swimming pool.

There were phones in every room except the bathrooms. We had two lines, one
for everyone, and one for family and very close friends. Evie logged countless hours
on behalf of Van, and also stoked the social fires, organizing lavish parties and film
screenings. The house included a projection room and a movie screen hidden behind
a leather and cork scene of the African veldt.

Evie actually loved managing Van's career, planning vacations and arranging
summer activities for us. She ran the house, including the household help, smoothly,
and kept up with all of their friends, as well as ours. We took piano lessons, and I

Friends Peter
Lawford, Lucille
Ball and Van
Johnson at the
premiere of *The
Yearling*, 1946.

KISSING *and* CUSSING
IN THEIR HAPPIEST,
SCRAPPIEST ROMANCE!

Metro-Goldwyn-Mayer *and* Liberty Films Present

**SPENCER TRACY
KATHARINE HEPBURN
VAN JOHNSON**
ANGELA LANSBURY
ADOLPHE MENJOU · LEWIS STONE
FRANK CAPRA'S
**STATE OF THE
UNION**

took ballet lessons and horseback riding. Evie had her own
secretary, and together they worked on Van's schedules,
the party and birthday invitations, the Christmas card list,
and activities for us kids—including summer camp. Van
and Evie traveled a great deal during those months, thus
necessitating the camps, which we all hated. (At the age
of 8, I was locked in a closet at Marymount summer camp
when I cried for my mother. It's no surprise, after three
weeks of hell, that I was emotionally unable to stay the
entire term, and was allowed to go home early.)

Evie also handled unpleasant duties for Van, including, on one occasion,
turning down Desi Arnaz for *The Untouchables*. As much as Van
actually disliked making movies (preferring the theater), television
was the absolute limit; he abhorred even the thought of it. As
sweet and ingratiating as Evie was, Desi was furious, causing a
permanent rift in the friendship.

✦ ✦ ✦

The parties were large, loud, long and exciting; Judy Garland
sang and Leonard Bernstein played the piano, and usually the
evenings ended peacefully. But one night Rhonda Fleming was
there, with every man at the party surrounding her; predictably,

Van Johnson starred with Judy Garland in the 1949 MGM remake of the film *In the Good Old Summertime,* which was directed by Robert Z. Leonard (and an uncredited Buster Keaton).

SONGS!

TECHNICOLOR!

JUDY GARLAND
VAN JOHNSON
Fall in Love
IN THE GOOD OLD
SUMMERTIME MGM

S.Z. SAKALL · SPRING BYINGTON   A ROBERT Z. LEONARD PRODUCTION

the adulation ended in a huge fight. I saw a crowd of people in the entry hall and Evie ineffectually dancing around the perimeter trying to stop it. From my bedroom window I heard some men muttering darkly about what they planned to do in a sneak attack, and I yelled down, "I'm calling the police!" They scattered.

We always had a cook; our favorite was Delphine, a wonderful woman from Haiti, who made us special treats including a choo-choo train made entirely from lemons, and our favorite, a loaf of chocolate wafer cookies interspersed with heavy cream, which she froze—it was to die for. When I didn't eat my vegetables or was difficult, she fashioned a little gnome out of twigs, which she put in the tree outside our kitchen; the sight of it was sufficient to inspire me to do anything I was told.

Evie was a fabulous cook and would sometimes do the cooking herself; no one could make gravy the way she made it, or roast a leg of lamb the way she did. One of Van's favorite breakfasts was cinnamon toast, served in a toast rack, along with scrambled eggs and bacon.

Both Van and Evie had a sweet tooth, and we always had chocolates and huge jars of hard candy. A special drawer in the kitchen was filled with fresh donuts, and cakes and pies. Van loved licorice allsorts and circus "peanuts," which were orange-colored and banana-flavored marshmallow. He also fancied chocolate bark from Edy's Candy Roundup, a nearby shop. One of our special treats was going to Wil Wright's Ice

Cream Parlor, accompanied by our boxer, Joey, who always got his own ice cream cone, which he gobbled on the sidewalk.

Back at home, Joey, Van and I would pile onto Van's bed—an oversized king specially made by the actor-turned-furniture-maker George Montgomery—with candy everywhere. We watched *The Honeymooners*, as Van adored Jackie Gleason, and the *Million Dollar Movie*. One time the featured film was the thriller *The Spiral Staircase*, and we watched it all week long. It scared me to death, but I felt safe with Van there.

Before the start of a new picture, Van would diet furiously, but if we were watching television and a beer commercial would come on, showing a tall, frosty glass with moisture running enticingly down its sides, I would be dispatched to our bar downstairs for a six-pack. One night Van took me to dinner at Perino's, and we tried to be good, but a basket of thin, crispy toast with garlic butter was placed on the table, and good intentions melted away.

More "snapshots" of the Johnson house: I won a duck in a school raffle and brought it home in a box; Evie was less than thrilled, but Van loved it. I would

Although he was unable to serve in the military, Van Johnson played many military roles, such as in the MGM film *Battleground* (1949).

Actress Joan Crawford visits Van Johnson on the set of the film *Easy to Love*, circa 1953.

come home from school and find Van happily sailing Dudley in the swimming pool. (We eventually gave Dudley to the milkman, who had a small farm; later Dudley had ducklings and was renamed.) Another time Van found Tracy planting a package of hot dogs, one by one, in hopes of growing a hot dog tree.

During the Great Bel Air Fire in 1961, I packed a suitcase with my favorite books and toys and headed out for the pool; I heard a low chuckle and there was Van, watching me from the upstairs porch. He gently told me we were okay, safe, and that the fire would not reach us.

Van cherished his privacy and despised autograph seekers—especially when they interrupted a meal. One morning we were having breakfast in the dining room when we heard tapping on the window; there were several people standing in the flowerbed! I thought Van was going to have a stroke.

ON THE ROAD, TRAVELING TOGETHER

Van loathed making movies—waiting for shots to be set up, waiting for lines to change, and the multiple takes all took a toll—but he came alive when performing onstage. He would revive himself in the summers by touring New England doing summer stock. One year it was *Damn Yankees*, the next, *Night Must Fall;* in the role of "Danny," he was fabulous. He needed the immediate feedback he got from a live audience. The attention energized him. These summer stock trips were in the late 1950s and included Tracy, Evie, Van and I; Ned stayed at home with his friends.

I wouldn't have missed them. It might've been during one of these trips when we were staying at the Plaza in New York City, waiting for room service. Van told us a story about Wallace Beery's first job as assistant elephant trainer, a job that required "unpacking," as in getting them ready for the show. Somehow he made us so hysterical with laughter that when room service arrived, none of us could speak, so hard were we gasping for breath.

I certainly did not have ordinary vacations. In 1954, I went to Honolulu to be with

Evie and Van Johnson, Janet Leigh and Tony Curtis arriving in Hawaii for the filming of *The Caine Mutiny*, circa 1954.

BIG AS THE OCEAN!
THE CAINE MUTINY

Van and Evie while they were on location for the film *The Caine Mutiny*. Stevie Bogart was there too with his parents. We played on the beach together. Van and Bogart were always dressed in kimonos when off duty. Once, Stevie and I were playing with matches under some palm trees on the beach and a shadow came over us; it was Bogart. He was angry but never raised his voice; he just told us we were never to play with matches again. That was the end of that.

We stayed at the Hôtel du Cap in Antibes, France in 1957, while Van was rehearsing for the *The Pied Piper of Hamelin*, a television movie that included music by Edvard Grieg. That summer was magical for me—the hotel was incredible, the Grieg music wafted through the air, and we cruised along the Mediterranean coast on a yacht that put in for dinner and then headed right back out again. We had our own area on the hotel grounds overlooking the sea, and one day we were sitting around when Gary Cooper came by. *Friendly Persuasion* was my favorite film, and I had seen it several times. When I asked him, "Are you the Gary Cooper who was in *Friendly Persuasion*?" he laughed and said yes.

One afternoon the Shah of Iran came to visit. He and Van were talking in our cabana while I was snorkeling for sea urchins. All of a sudden I felt the most incredibly

A film still from MGM's *The Last Time I Saw Paris* (1954) showing Van Johnson and his co-star Elizabeth Taylor.

painful stinging; I had swum into a school of jellyfish. I could see nothing, but I screamed from the shock and pain. Van was furious—he thought I was being naughty and playacting—but the Shah thought differently and dove in to carry me to safety. My legs were swollen to twice their size; someone poured kerosene over them, and I felt better immediately.

The France trip was actually our second visit with the Shah; the first was in Sun Valley in 1954 when Van was shooting *Duchess of Idaho* with Esther Williams. We were told to curtsy and bow, as he was a king. My brother Tracy bowed, looked at him and said, "If you're a king, where's your king's hat?"

In 1958, we stayed at the beautiful Hôtel des Trois Couronnes, overlooking Lake Geneva in Vevey, Switzerland. We were there looking at boarding schools for Tracy and me. While we usually ate in the hotel dining room, occasionally we ventured further afield. We had fabulous dinners across the street at a little sausage and cheese place, served by a wonderful woman named Armanda. Once Van ordered ice-cold beer with his fondue, and she cautioned him against it, stating cold beer and hot cheese would form a rock in his stomach. "Don't worry about me," Van replied, "I've got a cast iron stomach!" He was sick all night.

Despite making a bad call that time, Van had a strong sense of justice. He, Tracy and I were having lunch outside on the hotel patio when a woman came up to our table and started berating Van for having brought Tracy out in public. I was 10; Tracy was 13 and experiencing some adolescent acne. She told Van he had spoiled her lunch. He waited until she paused for a breath, and then he put down his fork, looked at her and said, "Madam, my son's face will clear up and he will be very handsome, but you will be ugly all your life." She left without another word.

Another day during the same trip, Evie, Van, Tracy and I went to visit Charlie Chaplin at his beautiful house, Manoir de Ban, to have lunch. I remember being so disappointed; I expected to meet "The Little Tramp" instead of this white-haired elderly gentleman, having made no allowance for the passage of time. He was very gracious, and I got to sit to his right at the table.

Van Johnson and his daughter, Schuyler, in Switzerland.

We also saw a lot of Noel Coward and his companion, Cole Lesley, whom we all called "Coley." They too had a house in Vevey. Noel was much amused by my moodiness and promptly christened me "Scowler." He was a brilliant raconteur, of course, and we had many pleasant times together.

At Christmas one year we stayed with Irene Wrightsman, of Standard Oil fame, at her chalet in Gstaad, named Les Trois Ours. I spent many weekends with Irene after that first visit. When I would leave to go back to St. George's—my boarding school— she would give me huge Steiff stuffed animals, including a big fish I could barely hold and, another time, a gorgeous teddy bear. The matron at school confiscated these lovely gifts, never to be seen again. Zsa Zsa Gabor came to visit me at the school one day and gave me a huge wicker hamper stuffed with goodies. That too was confiscated.

LONDON

When Van was performing in *Music Man* in London around 1960, the family went there as well. Our first flat was on Mount Street, and it was fabulous. My bathroom was bigger than my bedroom at home; it had two levels and heated towel racks—I was floored. But I practically lived at the Adelphi Theatre; eventually I knew the entire play by heart. Almost every night after the show, Van and I would walk across the back alley to Rules, the city's oldest restaurant. I would order the same thing night after night: grilled liver and onions.

Then we relocated to Kensington to a more modern flat—not nearly as nice, but very comfortable. One night it got really late and there was no sign of Van. Suddenly we heard his distinctive laugh floating up from the street; a friend had brought him home after a glorious night of drinking his new favorite treat—shandies, a blend of beer and bitter lemon. They went to the wrong floor, and when the door opened, a very old woman was standing there. Van looked at her and said, "Evie, you've changed!"

One rare day when Van was free, we went to see *The Amorous Prawn*, a popular stage comedy, which was hilarious. During one scene Van laughed so hard—he had a very infectious laugh—he literally stopped the show. He had fallen out of his aisle seat and was rolling around on the floor. The actors on stage began to laugh, and then the whole audience got going. It was several minutes before the play could resume.

While we were in London, Van took me horseback riding every week; he had an enormous black horse named Patience and I had a little pony called Sunshine. We went to Miss Dixon's stables in the Kensington Mews, decked out in full English riding gear—jodhpurs, velvet hard hats, boots, tweed jackets—and we carried riding crops, which we never used. Van and I would ride from Miss Dixon's to Hyde Park—just across the street— and we had a grand time trotting along "Rotten Row," a broad track running along the south side of the park. During the 18th and 19th centuries, Rotten Row was a fashionable place for upper-class Londoners to be seen. Today you can still ride horses there, but not many people do.

Speaking of the upper class, Queen Elizabeth and her sister, Princess Margaret, attended a performance

A clip from a London paper published while Johnson was performing in *The Music Man*.

MEN ABOUT TOWN
by PETER CLARKE

6. VAN JOHNSON

Star of "The Music Man," he is 43 years old and addicted to scarlet socks which have become something of a trade-mark. He says, "I never take this acting business too seriously. Deep down I'd much rather be running a hamburger stand on Cap d'Antibes." He is a great believer in astrology and a great disbeliever in psycho-analysis, and claims to be the only actor in Hollywood never to have seen the inside of a head-shrinker's office. He also says "If I had another life to live, I wouldn't be an actor again for all the beans in Boston."

THE CARLTON TOWER

Moon Girl— Loved your letter— You write so well— & Miss Lapidus was thrilled with her letter too— I'm glad you liked the booties! Ethel Toffemeyer cooked A huge turkey last night & invited Lily & her brother, Ruth Kettlewell, Bob Merryman, me, & C. Denny Warren & his wife— Pumpkin Pie for dessert!

Cadogan Place, London, S.W.1 / Telephone: BELgravia 5411 / Cable Address: Hocoam London

...as. so good to have ...king again— the ...ts & decorations are ...ou Regent & Oxford ...I'm taking the kids ...between shows to— ...the last supper— back in town— ...me to lunch at ...Mirabelle — Isn't that interesting— Keep smiling & let me know when your holiday starts— Love— Daddy ☺

BY AIR MAIL
PAR AVION

Miss Schuyler Johnson
St. George's School
Clarens
Switzerland

ARE YOU ON
NEW VOTERS LIST
CHECK

Van often wrote quick letters to Schuyler when she was at school—
letters that were appreciated because they were filled with fatherly love.

of *Music Man*, and subsequently Van and Evie were invited to tea at Buckingham Palace. And one memorable night, Van, Evie and I went for dinner at the house of the Duke and Duchess of Beaufort at Badminton in Gloucestershire, where the famous game was invented. They had a pack of Pekingese dogs that I was enchanted with, and I asked, "Mrs. Duchess, may I please have one of those dogs?"

Another time, we went to Ascott House near Buckinghamshire, a vast estate of over 3,200 acres, and the family home of Evelyn de Rothschild. As you drove up to the house, there were humongous topiary chess pieces waiting for the start of a game. The view from the dining room was of meadows with sheep grazing in the distance—a painting come to life.

HOLLYWOOD LIFE, LATER

After our last trip to Switzerland in 1960, Van never came back to Foothill Road. The house was irrevocably changed—most of the rooms were dark, and there were no parties, no laws or rules, and no security at all. I remember a horde of young boys from Hollywood talent agent Henry Willson's stable descending on the house, charming my mother and then stealing everything in sight, drinking up all the liquor and eating our food. I stayed in my room with the door locked. They took all of Evie's handmade gowns, our antiques and anything else of value. It was horrible—like Georgia during Sherman's March.

There was still quite a collection of movie star kids on the Marymount school bus: Tina Sinatra, Mark Harmon, Jayne Marie Mansfield, and Lucie and Desi Arnaz Jr. Tina's parents were divorced at the time, and I remember her sadness; I wanted to help her but didn't know her very well.

My brothers and I knew Candace Bergen; we called her Candy. She dated Ned and Tracy and was friends with me. One day I went to her house in Brentwood, where she kept a white donkey. She took me into her parents' bedroom and pulled a leather suitcase out from under the bed; lo and behold, there was Charlie McCarthy. We weren't allowed to touch at all, and, of course, we were not even supposed to be doing what we were doing. (When her father, Edgar Bergen, had come to *our* house, he would do an act—painting his hand and putting a tiny scarf over it, and voilà, a little old lady. He made her talk and sing and come to life; she was fabulous.)

At a party at George Hamilton's house—an enormous estate that had been built by Douglas Fairbanks Sr. in 1919 (the year was engraved in the fireplace)—I was seated next to Gloria Swanson. It was the early 1960s. She graciously reenacted her staircase scene from *Sunset Boulevard* for me, while the party swirled around us. She said, "I suppose your friends think I'm nuts," to which I replied, "Oh, no, Miss Swanson, they admire you," which was true. Her face fascinated me; not a single line or wrinkle, just smooth glowing skin.

(Years later when we had the house to ourselves, Bill Hamilton, George's brother, and I explored the basement looking for the secret entry to Pickfair, which Fairbanks had built to connect the two houses so he and Mary Pickford could be together without being seen. We discovered that the tunnel in the basement opened up into the fireplace in the main house, but we had to turn back due to rats.)

Groucho Marx's daughter Melinda and I were also friends. Groucho took us with him golfing; he wore plus fours, argyle socks and a large tam o' shanter. He walked with his famous crouch throughout the course. He also took a group of us to Disneyland one time to see the circus attraction; he was wonderful to us, and, of course, very funny. A story circulated once that when Melinda went as a guest to a "restricted" country club, she was ordered out of the pool when the manager discovered she was Jewish. Groucho later called the manager and said, "My daughter's only half Jewish; is it okay if she goes in up to her waist?"

This was all around the time of Van and Evie's separation and drawn-out divorce, and my friends' famous parents were all very kind to me. There was a members-only discotheque in Beverly Hills in the 1960s called The Daisy, and one night Dean Paul Martin came to pick up Ned and me in a limousine to take us there, even though I was maybe 14. I had a huge crush on Dino, as he was known. We were sitting at our table when Johnny Carson came over and asked me to dance; we had a great time doing the twist. I remember him yelling (because it was so loud), "You sure shake a mean leg out here in L.A!"

During the Beatles' first trip to the United States in 1964, I was invited to a meet and greet at the home of Capitol Records executive Alan Livingston. I was 15. I shook hands with the band and had my photo taken. The next day I baked a banana cake, and took it to the house where they were staying in Bel Air. Evie was at the wheel and got us past the security guards. Our housekeeper, Mary Luke, and I went to the back gate with the cake while Evie waited in the car. Brian Epstein came out and told me to come in and give it to the group myself. Mary and I went in and spent an hour conversing with John, Paul and, later, Ringo, who came in wearing full cowboy regalia, six-shooters, chaps, boots and hat. George stayed in the dining room reading a book. They were interested in Van; they had seen him in *Music Man* and loved it. When we left—by the front door—there were literally thousands of fans being held back by police; they let out a roar, which scared me to death. No one believed that I had spent time with the Beatles. Evie had to verify the event.

I met Burt Lancaster in 1966 when I visited his son Bill at their house. Bill and I attended high school together, and I had no idea who his father was for several months. I spent a lot of time with Bill and Burt. Burt and I would go to UCLA to exercise; we would do the Perrier run (an obstacle course) or just run on the track. Once, after running, we went to get our gear, and there were a couple of guys on their hands and knees looking for a contact lens. We were helping them when the one who'd been staring at Burt said, "Kirk Douglas," to which Burt replied, "Yes."

With my new driver's license, I drove Burt to the airport on several occasions. Once he invited me to wait with him in the VIP lounge; he got very excited when he spotted Merle Oberon seated nearby. On a trip from New York to Los Angeles, he was over the moon when he was seated next to Bob Dylan. Burt wasn't one for dressing up; when his daughter Susan and I once drove him to the airport, he was wearing an old Mexican serape and sweatpants held together with a safety pin. He had packed his things into two pet carriers each with printing on the side that read, "I'm feeling better now." Two ladies were staring at him and said, "That looks like Burt Lancaster, but it couldn't be."

Burt owned part of an exclusive nightclub in L.A. called The Factory. When several of our group went there to go dancing, including his youngest daughter, Sighle (pronounced "Sheila"), the doormen refused to let us in because we were wearing Levis. Sighle called her father, and half an hour later Burt showed up wearing Levis.

After his divorce, Burt lived in a fabulous house in Malibu, and a group of about twenty of us, including Burt's children and friends, were usually there every weekend. One Saturday I had arrived before anyone else, and the doorbell rang; when I answered, it was Shelley Winters. She was wearing a baseball cap and was very loud and stressed, demanding to know where Burt was.

✦ ✦ ✦

Despite both of my parents having theater backgrounds, I was never an actor myself. In the early 1970s, I had my own interior plant business. I received a call from an elderly lady, Miss Helm, requesting my services. After I asked for directions, there was a pause, and then she said, "It's Pickfair." I was awestruck upon finally seeing the interior of the famous estate. The entry hall had a genuine Old West saloon complete with bar, spittoons, tables and chairs, and beautiful old paintings. Upstairs was a huge living room with a fireplace, and the dining room had glassed-in areas containing a set of dishes once belonging to Napoleon and etchings by Michelangelo. Buddy Rogers greeted me and was very gracious; he had tears in his eyes when he explained that his wife, Mary Pickford, never came downstairs any more.

Mary Pickford was the queen of silent films, and later wife to movie idol Buddy Rogers. Here is a Christmas greeting from holiday time.

I always wore white gloves to church, and was told many times that if I wore white gloves, like Grace Kelly, I too would marry a prince. I believed it, but sadly, he never showed up.

Evie was not perfect by any means, nor were any of us; but she was always a loving mother, a source of safety and security, and one you could go to for anything and not be disappointed.

What follows is my mother's scrapbook and original photo captions. She worked on her scrapbook from 1999 until she got ill in 2003. She did not want to write a book, per se, just captions for her photographs. She started taking pictures in 1953 and never stopped. She was an avid shutterbug. She had several cameras, from a tiny Minox, to a three-lens Stereo Realist for her slides, to a Polaroid, to a Kodak Brownie. After a long illness, at the age of ninety, Evie passed away.

I did have a correspondence of sorts with Van, and he continued to send me books, but for all intents and purposes, that part of my life was over. I only saw him twice afterwards; once at the Polo Lounge in 1966 for lunch (he gave me a copy of *Rosemary's Baby),* and one more time at the Boca Resort in 1996—I was 48—when he was in town to do a charity appearance. I didn't call first, I just showed up. He was polite but stressed, as he always was before an appearance. We conducted our conversation as he held the door open only slightly, holding a mascara wand in his other hand—his lashes were very light. He said he would call me. He never did, and I don't know much about his life behind that door, but just having seen him made me feel content.

Evie Johnson put her and her family's life—and practically all of Hollywood's—into a scrapbook she titled "The Fabulous Life of a Hollywood Wife...As Seen through My Camera."

The Fabulous Life of a Hollywood Wife...

as Seen Through My Camera

By Evie Wynn Johnson

BY EVIE WYNN JOHNSON

Here is a great group photo of "aspiring starlets." This would have been taken in the late 1920s or early '30s. Can you locate Edna Marion, Dolores Del Rio, Fay Wray, Mary Brian, Sally O'Neil, Janet Gaynor and Mary Astor? Of course, the lady in the first row center is Joan Crawford. [1926]

EARLY DAYS

Here is my lifetime friend and lover, Tyrone Power, in a scene from the 1936 Broadway production of *Saint Joan*. This was a very young Ty Power, and before his Hollywood stardom. Here he is with the great actress Katharine Cornell.

When Ty and I first met and started dating, we were in *Romeo and Juliet*, starring Katharine Cornell, Maurice Evans and Ralph Richardson, in 1935. When this was taken in 1938, he was shooting *Suez*. I was staying with him in Bel-Air, California, for the summer.

yrone Power and I, at the beach in Ensenada, Mexico, taken in
1938. Ty was my first love, and I his. One of the finest people I
have ever known—women were attracted to him like bees to honey.
I also think he was underrated as an actor because he was so handsome. He did manage to get some "meaty" roles, including *Lloyd's of
London, The Rains Came, The Razor's Edge* and one of my favorites,
The Eddy Duchin Story. Ty also distinguished himself in the Marines
during World War II as a highly decorated pilot.

This snapshot of Jan Sterling, Ty and myself was taken at his pool circa 1945.

Tyrone and I maintained a very close relationship throughout our lives; here we are conferring with some models at a fashion show.

A study in profiles? French actress Annabella, Ty Power and myself. It is very obvious who is the more beautiful!

Ty Power sent me this picture of him and his friend Watson during World War II.

An early picture of [first husband] Keenan and me taken in Skowhegan, Maine, with his father, Ed Wynn. We were performing in summer stock, 1939.

This was taken when we lived in the house at 216 Saltair. My son Ned, Keenan and I are "posing" on Keenan's motorcycle. He loved riding, and this was before he was involved in a terrible motorcycle accident. In 1945, Keenan was hospitalized for three months. Obviously, I never liked motorcycles, and always worried when he rode them.

Here are three generations of Wynns: Tracy on the left, Ed Wynn next to him (the proud grandfather), then Edmond Keenan Wynn [Ned] between Ed and Keenan, on the occasion of Ned's 21st birthday.

Grandfather Ed Wynn, father Keenan Wynn, and son Ned Wynn, along with Jerry Lewis— comedians all. Jerry was popular in the United States, but the French critics and public revere him as one of the "greats." Jerry would agree with that accolade.

A threat to Lunt and Fontanne? Keenan and I are "serious thespians" in this 1939 photograph. We were both appearing in Broadway plays when this was taken.

OPPOSITE

(*top*) Very rare photo of Marlene Dietrich and her husband, Rudi Sieber, taken at our [Keenan and my] house; Marlene was our neighbor when I was married to Keenan. Our son Ned is in the picture with our poodle, Coco. (*bottom*) Marlene Dietrich sent me this letter while she was overseas with the troops.

No. 950751

[CENSOR'S STAMP]

To Mrs. KEENAN WYNN
BIRCH WOOD DRIVE
LOS ANGELES 24
CALIF.

From MARLENE DIETRICH
U.S.O. ENTERTAINER
(Sender's name)

A.P.U. 782 NEW YORK CITY
POSTMASTER
(Sender's address)

4/11/44/c
(Date)

Hello Darling — this is a wonderful
life. It's beautiful here and
I am happy — sunshine and
wonderful people. I met a friend
of mine here. Everybody is so
kind to me that I almost can't
take it. We will leave here soon
Please write — love to everbody
kiss Ned and Keenan. Marlene
Hello! it is wonderful I am Happy
all Love   Jean (JEAN)

V - MAIL

English liberated Prisoners

OPPOSITE & ABOVE

The wonderful pictures Marlene Dietrich sent me in 1944, when I
was married to Keenan. She was overseas at the time, entertaining
the soldiers "somewhere in Europe." Marlene was a very dear friend
and volunteered her time for the love of her country, America. She
loved entertaining the troops, and they loved her.

Keenan and I in the pool at the house of Desi Arnaz and Lucille Ball, when they were first married and living in the Valley. The pool was built, as you can see, to resemble an old swimming hole with no steps, and necessitated pulling yourself out by a rope. Great fun. Circa early 1940s.

Here I am "on my mark" between two acting "giants." This is Keenan, myself and the very talented actor Laird Cregar. His Hollywood career lasted a brief five years due to his early death at 31 from a weakened heart. He was so memorable in *The Lodger* and *Hangover Square*—a fine talent. This picture was taken at Ty Power's pool.

When I was married to Keenan, we bought a house on Saltair in Brentwood. We didn't know it at the time, but Rocky and Gary Cooper lived across the street. We had been in the house a few days when the doorbell rang; when I opened it, there stood Gary Cooper and his wife, Rocky. I thought I was going to faint. They came to welcome us and had brought wine, bread and salt for good luck. We were overwhelmed by such a warm welcome. We didn't have a pool on our property, so we went to the Coopers to swim and play tennis. Gary had a small, separate house where he kept his trophies and hunting gear. One night, after dinner, Gary came into the main house and said, "Evie, I want to show you something." He was pointing this long cylindrical weapon (which was some sort of rifle) in my direction. I asked "What is that?" To which Gary replied, "This is a Civil War bazooka." I said, "Gary, that makes me nervous, I don't like guns, please turn it away from me…" He laughed and said, "Evie, it's over 100 years old and has no ammunition in it." With which he held it up, took aim, and it went off, missing me by a few inches, and blowing a huge hole in their brick fireplace. Gary was stricken, but I just laughed and said, "Glad the gun wasn't loaded." (Pictured: Keenan Wynn and Gary Cooper.)

*H*ere I am out for the
evening with two of my
favorite actors, Keenan Wynn
and Peter Lawford. The dress I
am wearing was very beautiful,
and designed for me by the
Fontana Sisters of Rome.

I took this picture of Van,
Mickey Rooney, Peter
Lawford and Keenan on the
diving board at our pool on
Devon, in 1942. I think it's
a great shot, don't you?

OPPOSITE

Van, Keenan and me in more halcyon
days: who could predict the future? I
sure couldn't! (Circa 1946.)

HOUSE OF STARS

The Johnson house, 801 North Foothill Road, Beverly Hills, 90210. Van and I lived here for 15 years and have many memories associated with our time spent under this roof. We had over an acre of land in the "flats" (very desirable) of Beverly Hills. Built in 1935, the house had a paneled elevator, which connected our library with our upstairs sitting room. There were five bedrooms upstairs, and the housekeeper's quarters were on the ground floor. There was a separate apartment over the four-car garage, and a separate laundry room on the side. Our oversized playroom contained our bar, and was a beautiful example of Art Deco, with the bar done entirely in copper, and the walls covered in leather with copper studs framing the sections; it also boasted a movie screen. The projectionist's room was outside and had its own entrance. A cork mural depicting the African veldt covered the movie screen and folded back when we ran our movies, which we did frequently for our guests and for the children and their friends.

A view of the back of the house.

*T*his was taken from our pool, and shows the back of the house and some of the backyard. We had several fruit trees, two of which— one lemon and one orange— were given to us as a fifth anniversary (wood) present from Mary Lee and Douglas Fairbanks, Jr. I thought the gift was very apropos.

H ere are three "girls" catching up on conversation.
This was a baby shower for Jimmy Stewart's wife,
Gloria. With her are Janet Gaynor and Ann Sothern.

OPPOSITE

Ravishing, redheaded actress Rhonda Fleming, surrounded by
her "entourage." Rhonda photographed beautifully in color, as
you can see here, and played a variety of leading-lady roles.

During the 1940s and
1950s, I had many
beautiful gowns designed for
me by well-known designers
of those decades. You can
see that I was quite happy
to be photographed wearing
some of them. My daughter,
Schuyler, appears happy also.

A St. Patrick's Day Party.

Gary Cooper, Peter Lawford and myself in our house on Foothill during the Van years. Gary, not a "yup" and "nope" man, was well educated and had attended Oxford in England. Here he is regaling us with funny stories.

Maureen Reagan, daughter of Ronald Reagan and Jane Wyman, and Van Johnson in the bar of 801 North Foothill Road.

Four very happy mothers at a baby shower. Left to right, they are: Mary Lee Fairbanks (married to Douglas Fairbanks, Jr.), Dinah Shore Montgomery, Evie Johnson (me) with daughter Schuyler, and actress Deborah Kerr Bartley.

This picture was taken at the Empire Theatre in London, England, November 1951. I was presented along with Van Johnson and a number of Hollywood stars to the Queen of England, Elizabeth, who later became the beloved Queen Mother. At the time, the King was too ill to attend. Also presented were Burt Lancaster, Dan Duryea and Ben Lyon, a film star from the 1920s and 1930s. I was told that, at that time, I was the only wife of a movie star to ever be presented to royalty, and I felt very honored.

ROYALTY

November 5, 1951. This picture was taken at a Royal Command Performance at the Empire Theatre in London, where I was presented to the Queen of England, later affectionately referred to as the Queen Mum.

Being presented at the same time were Burt Lancaster, Dan Duryea and Fred MacMurray. I did a deep curtsy (as required by protocol) and was rising when the Queen looked at me and said, "Lovely, lovely." I was wearing a gown designed for me in Rome by the famous Fontana Sisters. It was a beautiful shade of shell pink, and was covered with pearls and rhinestones.

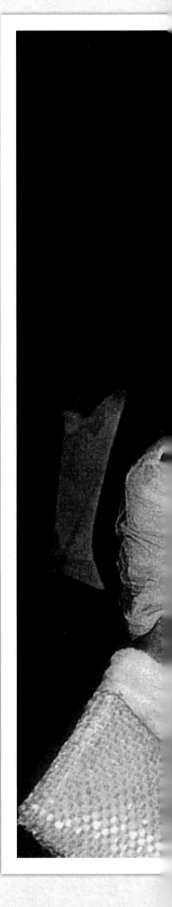

Audrey Hepburn: I snapped this in Antibes. I first met her at Claridge's in London, where we had tea with her and her mother. I wondered if she would continue to use the name Hepburn when she hit Hollywood, as there was another famous Hepburn at the time, Katharine. Since it was her real name, she said she had no intention of changing it, which I thought was very gutsy. She remarked: "I'll be a bigger star than Katharine Hepburn."

French actress Annabella, with the REAL Prince Michael Romanov.

Prince Ali Khan at his villa, L'Horizon, in Antibes. He was a charming host with a great sense of humor, and very down to earth.

Here I am sunning myself on Prince Ali Khan's yacht, somewhere on the French Riviera.

This is my son Edmond Keenan Wynn (Ned), me, Princess Ati [Fathia] (the sister of King Farouk of Egypt) and her husband, Rhyad Ghali. King Farouk had disowned her because of his disapproval of her husband, a "commoner"—a dislike that turned out to be justified in a terrible way. Princess Ati and her mother, Queen Nazli, had moved to Beverly Hills. King Farouk took care of Queen Nazli financially, as I often saw her darting in and out of stores on Rodeo Drive. Several years after this picture was taken, Princess Ati's husband was tried and convicted of her murder.

OPPOSITE

This is a picture I took after lunching with Lady Sylvia Ashley Gable, Phie Shepridge and Sita Devi, the Maharani of Baroda. Phie's husband, John, was the head of 20th Century Fox in England.

Here is Danny Kaye, in drag, doing his impression of Kay Thompson (at Ciro's—early 1950s). This was for some benefit. Note Jack Benny, Jack Carson, Van Johnson and George Burns behind Danny. Also, there's Jack Benny's wife, Mary, at a ringside table.

SOUNDS OF MUSIC

Here is dancer, singer and actor Bobby Van and his wife
at Ned's birthday party. Bobby was multitalented and
died at a relatively young age in 1980—only 51 years old.

I'll never forget Ethel
Merman at a party Cole
Porter was hosting for her.
Cole had a beautiful set of Baccarat crystal glassware.
He lifted the delicate stem glass to propose a toast and remarked, "This
glass would indent and then return to its original shape if squeezed very
carefully." Ethel, already three sheets to the wind, said, "Oh, what fun! Let
me try it." With which she picked up the fragile glass and squeezed it into
fragments. I thought Cole was going to have a stroke. He yelled, "Goddamn
it, Ethel, I am never going to invite you to another party..." It had been a
service for thirty-six, and now was only thirty-five...poor Cole!

The formidable and sometimes feared newspaper and radio columnist Walter Winchell sings with Frances Faye. Frances was a terrific entertainer of rather "suggestive" and risqué songs.

OPPOSITE

Interesting duo: June Allyson and Johnny Ray. In the early 1950s, Johnny was a big hit (on par with Elvis and Frank) with his rendition of "The Little White Cloud that Cried." I was amazed at the quality of his singing, as he was nearly completely deaf.

J udy Garland, enceinte, Dinah
  Shore and Linda Christian
discussing music with Roger Edens,
head of MGM's music department.
Edens won the Academy Award for
the scoring of *Easter Parade*.

J udy Garland and
  Ann Sothern in the
playroom, circa 1954.

Judy Garland and Janet Gaynor, the two stars of *A Star is Born*—Janet in the 1937 version and Judy in the 1954 production—reminiscing about their roles. Janet was a lovely woman and talented artist who excelled in renderings of onions so realistic, your eyes would water just looking at them.

Judy Garland singing at one of our parties.

Playroom/projection room. A picture of Schuyler (blue sweater) with Liza Minnelli and Melinda Marx, Groucho's daughter. We ran the latest Disney movies at our house—always a big hit with the younger set.

Van at MGM with Little Stevie Wonder playing the piano. Stevie was about four years old and already a child prodigy.

took this picture of my daughter, Schuyler, meeting the Beatles on their first visit to America in 1964, at a garden party given by Alan Livingston, record producer at Capitol Records. The next day I drove my daughter and our wonderful cook, Mary, armed with a freshly baked cake, through the heavily guarded gates of Bel-Air, to the house the Beatles were staying at during their visit to California. After telling the guards we were on our way to visit Gene Kelly, we proceeded to drive to the Beatle house. Mary and Schuyler had a long and fascinating visit with the Fab Four, and a unique memory to share.

Yul Brynner, relaxing in our playroom, at our house on Foothill Road, 1956, during the filming of *The King and I*. Yul had tremendous charm and charisma.

OPPOSITE

Leonard Bernstein, Van and our two boxer dogs, Joe and Mamie, relaxing at our bar. The men, not the dogs. Leonard was a marvelous pianist/composer/conductor who wrote [the music for], among others, *West Side Story*.

Eddie Fisher, crooner, and Jule Styne, songwriter, entertain at a Hollywood party. That lovely blonde is Mal Milland, wife of actor Ray Milland. Also note the handsome gentleman in the background (left) is Cesar Romero, popular Hollywood escort and actor.

Van, Sammy Davis Jr. and I in Sammy's dressing room at the Sands Hotel in Las Vegas, after his car accident. Sammy was a huge talent, and we flew to Las Vegas expressly to see his act. He had lost his eye in the accident, but never lost his sense of humor or his zest for life.

Van and I visited with the legendary Broadway actress Katharine Cornell at her home at Snedens Landing ([on the] Hudson River). Here we are having lunch with Kit's husband, Guthrie, and her aunt. I first met Kit in 1935 when I was hired to play one of the "ladies-in-waiting" in her *Romeo and Juliet*.

HAPPY HOLIDAYS

ESTHER AND FAMILY
LORENZO, MICHELE, KIM,
TOM, BEN, SUSAN
AND THOMAS

MERRY CHRISTMAS

Mary

Christmas Wishes

Buddy.

Merry Christmas!
Happy New Year!
Oona + Charlie

TOP TO BOTTOM:

Christmas greetings from Esther Williams and family; from Mary Pickford and Buddy Rogers; from Oona and Charlie Chaplin.

Louis Jourdan and wife, Quique, at Palm Springs, 1951. Louis was an international film star who played many debonair Frenchmen, and was perfectly cast in *Gigi* and *Can-Can*.

I'm getting camera-ready next to Charlie Chaplin at his Switzerland home, Manoir de Ban. My son Tracy Wynn is on the right.

OPPOSITE
Lunch with Charlie Chaplin and family at his home in Vevey, Switzerland.

At lunch in Switzerland: Cole Lesley, Van Johnson,
Noel Coward, Schuyler Johnson and me.

OPPOSITE

I took this picture of Van at Doris Duke's house "Shangri La" in Diamond Head, Hawaii. He is pictured at her pool. One of the many extraordinary features of the house was the dining room, whose four walls were aquariums, almost as large as those at Sea World. Truly extraordinary.

Van and I at William Randolph Hearst's Castle, San Simeon, in 1948. I was having a difficult recovery from the Caesarean birth of my daughter, Schuyler. We had gone to Hawaii on the old *Matsonia* to help me recuperate. When we got there, Van was mobbed by fans to the point where we were forced to fly home two days later. Marion Davies, Mr. Hearst's mistress of many years, heard of this incident in the paper, and called to ask if I would like to recuperate at San Simeon, to which I replied, "Would I ever!" We had the fabulous Castle to ourselves for three weeks, along with a staff of twenty-six.

In front of the great pyramid at Giza, 1959. Van and I were on a junket with Conrad Hilton along with other Hollywood stars for the opening of his Nile Hilton Hotel. Pictured are Conrad, me and Nina Warren, whose husband was Earl Warren, then governor of California and later head of the Warren Commission, which examined the details of the assassination of John F. Kennedy.

On the junket I photographed actor Hugh O'Brian "clowning" with a camel. Hugh became a very popular television star in his role of Wyatt Earp.

OPPOSITE

I found this sweater with the camels appliquéd, which I thought very appropriate for the trip.

Rosalind Russell and I demonstrating the famous Hollywood "air kiss" for Roz's film

Dynamic Duos

"To Eve with love and affection" —Darryl F. Zanuck and wife Virginia on the occasion of their Golden Wedding Anniversary. Notice the many awards in the background—five Academy Awards.

Director Henry Hathaway and actor Ray Milland in our playroom. Henry was a terrific director, and Ray, who we called Jack, was a romantic leading man. He had great success with *The Lost Weekend* and, later, in *Dial M for Murder*.

OPPOSITE

Visiting with June Allyson on the set during the production of one of several pictures she made with Van—he, MGM's "boy next door," and Little June, their perennial "girl next door." The ostrich-feather hat I am wearing was a gift to me from Marlene Dietrich.

This is a wonderful picture of Dinah Shore and husband George Montgomery. He and Dinah were married for a number of years. George was a leading man of numerous Hollywood Westerns, but his "real" artistic talent was that of carpentry. He carved a bed for Van and me—it was seven feet by seven-and-a-half feet, king-sized—and it was hand turned, made of the most beautiful wood. He also made beds for the two boys, and for Schuyler, a four-poster. He made a beautiful canopy for our bed as well.

Van and Norma Shearer at a party in the 1950s. Norma was a huge star in the 1930s and '40s; she was billed as MGM's First Lady of the Screen. Norma was able (with the assistance of her husband, MGM production executive Irving Thalberg) to play a variety of roles, from *Marie Antoinette* to *Romeo and Juliet* to *The Women*.

I love this picture of my dear friend Rocky Cooper with Peter Lawford, taken at Rocky's house. Rocky was a great friend. Peter, a sweet guy who became a romantic leading man, was later known for being a member of the infamous Rat Pack as well as JFK's brother-in-law.

Henny and Jim Backus. Very dear friends of mine. I met Jim in 1936 when I was in Cleveland doing a radio show called *The Skidoo Lady,* and on the Ray Perkins Variety Show. Jim was the announcer, and we became friends and remained friends until his death in 1989. Jim was so versatile in *I Married Joan* and *Gilligan's Island,* and as the father of James Dean in *Rebel Without a Cause,* in addition to providing the voice for the nearsighted Mr. Magoo. Jim and his devoted wife Henny wrote several hilarious books, including *Rocks on the Roof, What Are You Doing After the Orgy?* and *Forgive Us Our Digressions.*

Young Tyrone Power Jr., my godson, whom Ty never saw. Tyrone died on November 15, 1958; his son was born January 19, 1959. When young Tyrone was born, we (Van and I) took him and his mother, Debbie, home from the hospital. I held the baby all the way home. When Ty Jr. and his wife [DeLane Matthews] had a son, they named him Tyrone Keenan Power, because of the great friendship between [my first husband] Keenan [Wynn] and Ty.

OPPOSITE

I appeared as a guest on Ann Sothern's popular television series, *Private Secretary.* I played Flame Frobisher, a vamp.

Two beautiful people who [were] married for a lifetime (by Hollywood standards!), Ricardo Montalbán (after great success as a Latin lover for MGM, Ricardo starred in the hit television series *Fantasy Island*) and his wife, Georgiana, the youngest half-sister of Loretta Young.

William (Bill) Powell and Bonita Hume (who was married to Ronald Colman) in our playroom. Bill, along with Myrna Loy, starred in the MGM series *The Thin Man*. He had been engaged to Jean Harlow and had been devastated by her untimely death. Bonita was a lovely English actress and great fun, as was Bill. After Ronald (remembered to this day for his performance as Sydney Carton in *A Tale of Two Cities*, notably for the line "T'is a far, far better thing I do than I have ever done; t'is a far, far better rest that I go to than I have ever known…" when he was on the scaffold) died, Bonita married George Sanders, who had been married to Zsa Zsa Gabor. We saw George and Bonita frequently when we were in Lausanne, Switzerland. George was an excellent composer and a talented musician.

anet Leigh and Tony Curtis on the *Lurline* going to Hawaii, early 1950s. Tony is best known for his brilliant comedic role opposite Marilyn Monroe and Jack Lemmon in *Some Like It Hot*; Janet, of course, famous for the shower scene in *Psycho*. Alfred Hitchcock, some years later, was engaged in conversation with a moviegoer who complained that since his wife saw *Psycho,* she refused to take a shower. Hitch paused and said, "Have her dry-cleaned."

Actor Tony Curtis and wife Janet Leigh, clowning for my camera.

Ann Sothern and Rock Hudson. I loved giving "theme parties."
This one had a St. Patrick's Day theme (as you can see by
Ann's headgear and the table décor). Circa 1952.

ay Wray (*King Kong*) with playwright Clifford Odets, who came to visit her when we were all doing summer stock in Skowhegan, Maine. In the summer of 1939, when this was taken, they were having a hot romance at the time.

My son Tracy Keenan Wynn with Alan Alda on the set of *The Glass House*, which Tracy wrote. He also wrote the screen adaptation of *The Autobiography of Miss Jane Pittman*, starring Cicely Tyson, for which he won his second Emmy, and wrote *The Longest Yard,* starring Burt Reynolds. He won another Emmy for the 1970s [TV movie] *Tribes*.

With Lana Turner in Palm Springs, circa 1943. A great friend and a wonderful personality; I miss her very much. We had met when I was in California visiting Tyrone in the summer of 1938. Lana and I became really good friends, and we saw a great deal of each other. She had a certain naiveté, a quality completely opposite from her screen persona… she was warm, loving, giving, with a wonderful sense of humor.

This is a picture of me and my best friend, Nancy Deere Wiman
Carter Wakeman Gardiner, affectionately called Trink. Her father
had been a very successful Broadway producer, Dwight Deere Wiman.
This was taken on the occasion of her 75th birthday, at her house in
Millbrook, New York, in August 1993. I never knew what the "Deere"
stood for, until we were driving past a John Deere dealer advertising
various [types of] farm machinery/equipment. As we passed, Trink
looked up toward Heaven and said, "Thank you, great-great-great-
great-grandfather." I had no idea until then that she belonged to the
John Deere family; I had known her for many years, and she had never
mentioned the fact. In our later years she was very kind to me, and I
cannot express my gratitude for her friendship and her kindness.

This picture was taken circa 1946; Lana Turner, Rory Calhoun and Peter Lawford watching me put on my lipstick. Lana sports a new coiffure and a new man (at the time), Rory.

LET'S PARTY!

Another evening on the town. From left: Rock Hudson, Gene Tierney, Van, Skip and Henry Hathaway and me at Ciro's.

With Noel Coward, Lady Sylvia Ashley and Van. Noel was a wonderful friend, and so multitalented—actor, singer, writer, pianist, novelist— he could do it all. He wrote many original songs, including "Mad Dogs and Englishmen." Lady Sylvia Ashley, who bore a remarkable resemblance to Clark Gable's beloved wife Carole Lombard, became Clark's wife in 1949, but the marriage lasted just a few years.

O ut for a Hollywood evening with two good friends, the
lovely Ann Sothern and very handsome Peter Lawford.

T he wonderful
British actor
Ronald Colman with
Sarah Churchill.
Ronald possessed one
of the most beautiful
voices ever heard on
film. Sarah Churchill
was an actress,
and daughter of
England's Sir
Winston Churchill.

Richard Whorf, Van, Tony Bartley, Ronald Reagan and I at the Stork Club, late 1950s. The last time I saw Ronnie, I was staying at the Waldorf in New York. There was a crowd of people in the street and cameramen circling someone, and I saw Ronnie in the center of all the activity. I yelled, he turned around, and the Secret Service men started to approach me; he said "I know her; I want to say hello to her." He gave me a big hug and said, "Hi, Evie," and then he was whisked away by the agents. I later found out that he was the presidential nominee for the Republican party, 1976, and I was overjoyed when he became the 39th President of the United States.

H appy times: Van and I toasting the Ambassador to the Court of St. James, Lewis Douglas, and wife Peg.

OPPOSITE

Cheryl Crane, showing her beautiful mother, Lana Turner, the latest steps at Ned's 21st birthday party in 1962.

Actor Peter Fonda, son of Henry and brother of Jane, with wife Susie, sharing thoughts with Keenan Wynn at son Ned's 21st birthday party bash.

A very happy couple: actor, director and producer Dick Powell with his wife, Junie. Dick started out as a "crooner" in films and then progressed to dramatic roles playing tough guys and private eyes.

André Dubonnet, owner of the famous wine company, and me, at André's villa, Du Beau, on the French Riviera, 1955.

This picture was taken New Year's Eve, 1976. Pictured are Lee Minnelli (wife of Vincente), Ann Miller and myself. We were engrossed in discussing sequined dresses…as you can see!

Here is Mike Romanoff, who made his mark in Hollywood as the owner of the famous Romanoff's restaurant. He went by "Prince Romanoff," even though it was well known that his title was a phony one. Here he is with his wife, Gloria, around 1956 at the Sands Hotel in Las Vegas.

Left to right: Virginia Zanuck, Kitty Carlisle and her husband, Moss Hart (of Rodgers and Hart). Virginia knew Darryl was a philanderer, but hung in there and took care of him in his last days, until he died. He was the great love of her life. Moss Hart was an author as well as a composer, and [at this writing] Kitty [was] still making appearances in New York. She was also a panelist on *To Tell the Truth*.

I took this picture of Darryl Zanuck by the pool at his Palm Springs house. He was Chief of Production at 20th Century Fox Studios and solely responsible for elevating the studio to a major force in the industry. He was also instrumental in making stars out of contract players, including Gene Tierney, Alice Faye, Betty Grable, Cesar Romero, Carmen Miranda, Dana Andrews, Don Ameche and, last but not least, Tyrone Power.

I took this picture of Humphrey Bogart and Van at a luau given for us when we were staying at the Royal Hawaiian Hotel in Honolulu, Hawaii. Van, Bogie and Fred MacMurray were filming *The Caine Mutiny,* and we all had a great time. Bogie has a great sense of humor and showed a softer side on this location. Who couldn't relax in Hawaii? (Early 1950s)

Comedian-singer Martha Raye greets 1950s teen idol singer Eddie Fisher, at the 21st birthday party for my son Ned Wynn.

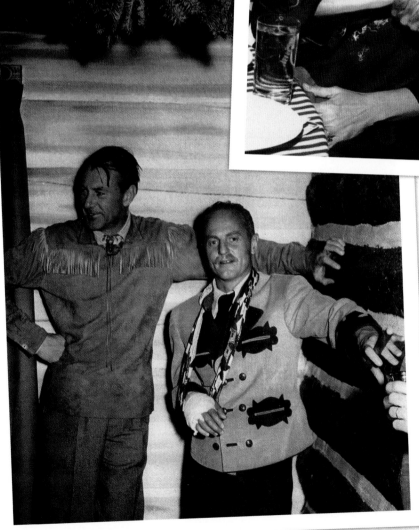

I took this photo of Gary Cooper and Darryl F. Zanuck in Sun Valley, after we'd just returned from skiing—Darryl with a broken arm, which he did not allow to interfere with his activities.

I think this is a "scoop": here is Joan Crawford with both Christina and Christopher, and the twins, all of whom she adopted. As everyone knows by now, she treated Christina and Christopher very badly, which Christina chronicled in her bestselling book *Mommie Dearest*, also made into a hit movie. Personally, I liked Joan very much as a hostess and a friend, rather than her mother persona. She was very good company, very kind to her friends, although some did not approve of her treatment of Christopher and Christina, who bore the brunt of her rages. By the time the twins came, she had mellowed significantly and was very good to them. When my son Tracy Keenan Wynn won an Emmy for *Tribes*, Joan sent him a letter on her famous blue notepaper. He wrote her a thank you note for her letter, to which she responded with another letter thanking him for this thank you note for her thank you note. She was very scrupulous with respect to her acknowledgment of her fans, and they responded by adoring her. She did whatever it took to retain her place in the Hollywood firmament, and was successful until her death.

I love this picture I took of Rocky Cooper, lifelong friend of mine, at her house in Holmby Hills, 1955. Wonderful hostess and more beautiful than most of the actresses of the time, she also possessed great taste, humor and kindness. A terrific athlete who excelled in swimming, tennis, golf, skiing and, last but not least, as a California women's skeet shooting champion.

In front of the fireplace in our playroom: the lovely Merle Oberon (Cathy in *Wuthering Heights* and Lady Marguerite Blakeney, wife of Sir Percy [Leslie Howard] in *The Scarlet Pimpernel)*. Great friend, health nut and a lot of fun.

Tony Curtis,
a little worse
for the bubbly.

This is one of the
many pictures
I took of my lifelong
friend and love, Tyrone
Power, circa 1949.

My dear friend Rocky Cooper with Sterling Hayden, at a dinner party in our dining room at Foothill, circa 1955.

Judy Garland, Charles Amory and Rocky Cooper at the Coopers' house, early 1950s.

OPPOSITE

Great profile shot of Norma Shearer, at a party in the mid 1950s. Behind her is husband Marti Arrouge; also James Woolf, an English producer, talking to Olivia de Havilland.

Van and I with Gloria and Jimmy Stewart, attending a play. I first met Gloria when I was in a play called *The American Way*; we had been introduced (in 1939) by a friend of hers who was in the show. Her name at the time was Gloria Hatrick. Jimmy, deeply in love with Gloria, was devastated when she died.

I took this picture of Roz [Russell] doing the "Limbo" at a party in Sun Valley; she's very "limber," as you can see.

Van, me and Ty at a party at Rocky and Gary Cooper's. Ty suddenly grabbed my leg and started kissing and biting it. At first Van smiled, and then he said, "I think that's enough."

Our playroom, circa 1952: Marilyn Morrison, daughter of Charlie Morrison, who owned the famous Mocambo nightclub; myself; and Tyrone Power. Marilyn was briefly married to Johnny Ray.

*B*eautiful Merle Oberon at a formal "do" flanked by Van and Noel Coward. Noel, of course, was one of Britain's most talented playwrights. He was a good friend through some rough times.

A party: Left to right, Graham Payn (a friend of Noel Coward's), Noel, [talent agent] Minna Wallis (Hal's sister), Van and Clifton Webb.

OPPOSITE

Van, Lana Turner, Laurence Harvey and Lex Barker at a party, circa 1954. Olivia de Havilland has her back to the camera.

Here is the Hearst columnist Louella Parsons. Her column was read daily by thousands of fans wanting "scoops" on the Hollywood stars. Here Louella is reading our cards...or are Van and I giving her a "scoop"?

Van and I with Esther Williams and her husband, actor Ben Gage.

Here's a wonderful picture taken on a junket to Washington, D.C. Here are (left to right), Paul Henreid, Alexis Smith, Reginald Gardiner, Angela Lansbury. In the front row are Eddie Bracken and two of MGM's most popular stars, Margaret O'Brien and Van Johnson, along with Diana Lynn. At the time, an MGM publicist told Van, "Stick close to Margaret O'Brien, and you will be photographed a lot." Obviously, Van took the publicist's advice.

ere I am with
Lex Barker,
who was the son of
a socially prominent
family. He played
Tarzan in five films,
and was married
five times.

The beautiful and
glamorous redhead
Arlene Dahl with her
"Tarzan," Lex Barker.
They were wed from
1951 to 1952, and Lex
later married another
ravishing beauty, my
friend Lana Turner. I
believe Mr. and Mrs.
Barker are costumed
for one of Lana's
Halloween parties.

*B*efore Mike Todd and Richard Burton, there was husband number two, English actor Michael Wilding, who is the father of Elizabeth Taylor's two sons.

The beautiful Elizabeth Taylor with her husband Michael Wilding and Van, taken at the Stork Club in New York. Michael was a prominent English actor and artist. On this particular evening, Michael started sketching Elizabeth on the tablecloth. He also included me looking on, watching him draw his lovely wife. I thought it was terrific and asked if I could have the sketch. He said, "Of course," so I called the headwaiter over and asked him to cut the tablecloth. I still have it, framed and hanging on one of the walls in my house.

Mike Todd, Elizabeth Taylor's third husband and the father of her daughter Liza. He was a terrific husband for Elizabeth, who needed someone very strong. We had gone to Louisville, Kentucky, for the premiere of her movie *Raintree County* with Montgomery Clift and Eva Marie Saint. This was taken in their room. Mike tried to persuade Van and me to fly to New York with him on his private plane, but we couldn't, due to a previous engagement, which saved our lives. The next thing I heard was that his plane had crashed; Van and I just looked at each other in stunned silence. What a loss.

Van Johnson, Yves Saint Laurent, Sophia Loren, William Powell and others at an event in Switzerland, circa late 1950s.

Actor Farley Granger makes a "point" in a conversation in our den. At one point, Farley spent so much time at our house that we named a bedroom "The Farley Granger Room."

Another picture of me with my father-in-law Ed Wynn at the Stork Club, New York City, 1940. He was unique, and like most comedians, he was rather dour offstage, but was extremely good to me and to Keenan. He regaled us with wonderful stories; one in particular has stayed with me. Ed was looking for investments that could provide a tax break; he met a man who told him that he owned some land in Brazil that was cheap and that Ed could buy and use as a plantation to grow crops. Ed was very interested, and said, "All right, how many acres and how much will it cost?" The man told Ed that for $5 an acre, he could get 10,000 acres, which Ed agreed to. Eventually Ed was forced to sue the man when he lost contact with him and his money.

When Ed took the stand, he told the judge what had happened, and that the land wasn't fit for farming; he said, "This man told me I could GROW nuts down there..." At that, the guy stood up and said to the judge, "No, sir, I said you could GO nuts down there."

THE COMEDIANS

He is my father-in-law and Keenan's father, Ed Wynn, a huge Broadway star and comic. Ed autographed this picture to me in 1938. He says, "To: Eve Abbott, in appreciation of her fine 'work' in 'Star Wagon'; may she stay on the 'Wagon' until she is a 'Star.'"

Another time in Hawaii, we met Eddie Cantor, a famous comedian of his day. We met during lunch at the Royal Hawaiian Hotel, 1953.

With George Jessel (the "Toastmaster General") and Jean Simmons, talented star of British and American films.

Everyone's favorite "Auntie Mame" and my dear friend, Rosalind Russell, relaxing in bed at Elizabeth Arden's Maine Chance Spa in Scottsdale, Arizona. Several times each year, Roz and I would book ourselves into this posh spa for recuperation and recovery from all the partying—exercises, mudpacks, facials and very good food (what there was of it.) Each year was more hilarious than the one preceding. One year Mamie Eisenhower was there; she had a bungalow near us with a private pool in between. No liquor, of course, was allowed, but late at night we would witness Mamie's maid sneak into the bushes and smash some empties.

Van, on our way to Honolulu, on the old ship *Matsonia*.
Van's idea of appearing "incognito." What do you think?

At one of Henny and Jim Backus's many parties; here I am with the wonderful George Burns. George was devastated when Gracie died, and drowned his sorrow in some wonderful films, e.g., *The Sunshine Boys* and *Oh, God!* We often discussed age and how old he was getting, and I told him my father was 90 plus, to which George replied, "Then I am going to make it to one hundred..." And he did. He had a very dry sense of humor, and was one of the sweetest men I've ever known.

Here are June Haver MacMurray, myself and the wonderful George Burns at a party at Jim and Henny Backus's house. George was a very funny man. Most comedians are not—most are rather dour when they are not onstage. I said to George, "But, you are not 'gloomy' off stage." To which George replied, "That's because I was the straight man. Gracie was the funny one."

I snapped this of voluptuous Jane Russell on one of a number of Hollywood junkets to publicize a film or opening of a hotel. She survived Howard Hughes's *The Outlaw*, and went on to play a number of cynical dames in movies.

Here's a wonderful profile shot of actor David Niven. He had the most wonderful wit and charm. His lovely wife, Primula Rollo, was fatally hurt at a Hollywood dinner party at Ty Power's house in Bel-Air. It was a Saturday evening and a black-tie affair. A game called "sardines" was played—a form of hide-and-seek—and apparently Primmie had mistaken a door to a lower-level cement garage for a closet, lost her balance and fell, and sustained a concussion. She was rushed to the hospital, where she died that night. Very sad and shocking.

I snapped this picture of Van, Judy Garland and daughter Liza on the set of 1949's *In the Good Old Summertime*. Little Liza made her screen debut in this one.

Van with Hattie McDaniel, smiling for the camera. Hattie won the Academy Award for her performance of Mammy in *Gone with the Wind* in 1939. Hattie broke the color barrier with her well-deserved awards.

Van Johnson signs autographs outside the restaurant Jack's at the Beach, in Santa Monica. Today, Van's fans are collecting signatures to ensure he'll be on the list of Hollywood stars featured on a future U.S. postal stamp. Bing Crosby, Jimmy Stewart, Judy Garland and Shirley Temple have already received their stamp; I think it's time for the boy next door.

Congratulations

by *CARLETON VARNEY*

Y ou may ask why I, along with Schuyler Johnson, decided to create this book about her parents, Van and Evie Johnson, more than 50 years after their marriage was over. Van never received an Oscar, like other stars who were not awarded the statuette—Marilyn Monroe, Errol Flynn, Doris Day, Richard Burton, Esther Williams, and Betty Grable, to name a few.

But Van Johnson represented the spirit of Hollywood in the '40s and '50s, the all-American matinee idol of the golden years. He was the dream of both mothers and of young ladies looking for their first boyfriend. He was the guy next door whom you wanted to be friends with—or actually be. When former MGM publicist and later agent to the stars Frank Lieberman saw Van and Evie being chauffeured through Palm Springs one sunny day in a white Cadillac convertible, along with baby Schuyler and her nanny, he thought, "Oh, God! How lucky can you get!" In real life, when not in front of the camera, Van was the man who knew everyone in Hollywood—and beyond. How could we not share these photos with you? Van was a pleasure to know... and his star will always shine brightly.

Van's star on the Hollywood Walk of Fame.

143

Van loved to paint and would start a canvas in the morning and have it completed by nightfall. The acrylics came right out of the tubes, and away went the brushes, creating dazzling sundrenched village scenes, landscapes and my favorite of all, bright, popping, colorful flowers.

BELOW

Painting was a passion. Van lived in an apartment with a big, big terrace and a small, small kitchen, and in another rented apartment, he enjoyed painting! Flowers, landscapes, still lifes—Van filled everything with magical color.

ABOVE

Shopping with Van for fabrics, furnishings and just about everything else—including red socks—was a dream come true for a Golden Age of Hollywood devotee like myself. Just remember, he was the "Pied Piper," and I, one of his followers. At home in his apartment on East 54th Street in New York City, he loved a cozy toile and everything that recalled pleasant days at Bailey's Beach in his hometown of Newport, Rhode Island.

RIGHT

Van and I going through the fabric sample racks at Carleton V. Ltd., our fabric and wallcovering showroom in New York City. Van loved to decorate.

Thursday

Carleton Bowes — Just
Returned San Antonio &
found your tasty present —
Yum-yum — I brewed a pot
of it wild — love cherries
anyway — I'm taping a thing
at Rossland next week with
June Allyson — after that
supper — shall we?
Thanks again — dear friend —
Big fat love to Suzanne —
Van —

To Carleton — ☺
Peace...! Van

Hi Carleton!
all good things To
you — Love —
Martin Williard

CITY OF NEWPORT

PROCLAMATION

WHEREAS, Van Johnson was born in Newport, Rhode Island on August 25, 1916 and was the son of Charles and Loretta Johnson who lived at l6 Ayrault Street; and

WHEREAS, Mr. Johnson attended Rogers High School and, after graduating, moved to New York City to pursue a career as an actor; and

WHEREAS, Mr. Johnson played on Broadway, working his way up from "chorus boy" to the lead in "Pal Joey"; and

WHEREAS, after Mr. Johnson was signed under contract to MGM, and his appearance in movies such as "A Guy Named Joe," and "Thirty Seconds Over Tokyo", the sensation he caused had "LIFE" Magazine declaring him "the most adored male in the U.S.", and The Saturday Evening Post calling him "The Bobby-Sox Blitzer"; and

WHEREAS, Mr. Johnson was so much more than a matinee idol. He was determined to be, and quickly became, recognized as a great actor. In film after film, he proved his ability to inhabit a character and shine through it; and

WHEREAS, Mr. Johnson left Hollywood in the late 50's with his family; his wife Evie, their daughter, Schuyler, and his two stepsons, Ned and Tracy Wynn and continued performing on the stage in New York, London and in summer stock to Standing Room Only audiences; and

WHEREAS, Mr. Johnson was highly regarded and even adored by those who worked with him and many testimonies to that fact abound; and

WHEREAS, Mr. and Mrs. Henry Shaffner are spearheading a campaign to have the United States Post Office issue a Van Johnson commemorative stamp paying tribute to Mr. Johnson; and

WHEREAS, the City of Newport is proud to be the birthplace of Mr. Johnson. **NOW THEREFORE BE IT**

RESOLVED: that I, Jeanne-Marie Napolitano, Mayor of the City of Newport in the State of Rhode Island and Providence Plantations, do hereby proclaim Tuesday, August 25, 2015, as

"VAN JOHNSON DAY"

in the City of Newport and call upon all citizens to join with me to celebrate the life and career of our beloved native son, Hollywood icon and legendary actor.

IN WITNESS WHEREOF, I have hereunto set my hand and caused the seal of the City of Newport to be affixed this 24th day of August in the year of our Lord 2015.

Jeanne-Marie Napolitano
Mayor

Newport, Rhode Island, may be famous for its mansions, but the city is always aware of its famous son Van Johnson, as it was on this proclamation day.